INTRODUCTION

Network marketing and direct selling are two of the most popular and lucrative business models in the modern economy. They provide individuals with the opportunity to build their own businesses and achieve financial freedom, without the need for significant capital investment or formal education. However, success in these industries is not guaranteed. It requires a combination of skills, strategies, and a willingness to work hard and persevere through challenges. In this e-book, we will explore the eight basic building blocks of network marketing and direct selling, and provide practical tips and insights on how to master them. Whether you are just starting out in network marketing, or you are a seasoned professional looking to take your business to the next level, this e-book will provide you with the tools and knowledge you need to succeed.

Here are eight basic building blocks of network marketing:

Dreams: Network marketing businesses should encourage their distributors to have big dreams and set goals for their business. This helps to motivate and inspire them to take action and build their business.

Commitment: Building a successful network marketing business requires commitment and dedication. Distributors should be committed to the company, product, and business opportunity.

Name list: The name list is a list of people that distributors know and can potentially approach about the business opportunity. It is important to have a large and diverse name list to maximize the potential for success.

Invitation and art of prospecting: Inviting people to learn about the business opportunity is a critical step in building a network marketing business. Distributors should develop their prospecting skills and learn how to approach people in a natural and effective way.

Presentation: The presentation is the process of sharing information about the company, product, and business opportunity with potential customers and distributors. It is important to have a clear and compelling presentation that communicates the benefits of the business.

Follow through: Following up with potential customers and distributors is important to keep them engaged and interested in the business opportunity. It is important to provide support and answer any questions they may have.

Counsel your upline: The upline is the person who recruited the distributor and is higher up in the network marketing organization. Distributors should seek guidance and support from their upline to help them build their business.

Duplication: Duplication is the process of teaching and training others to replicate the success of the distributor. It is important to have a simple and effective system that can be easily duplicated by others to help them achieve success in the business

CHAPTER 1

DREAMS

Dreams are a fundamental part of human existence. They are the things that we aspire to, the goals we set for ourselves, and the visions we have for our future. Dreams can be big or small, personal or professional, but they all represent the possibilities that exist in our lives.

From a human perspective, dreams are essential because they give us a sense of purpose and direction. They inspire us to push beyond our limitations and achieve our full potential. Dreams give us hope, motivation, and a reason to get up every day and work towards something that matters to us.

One example of a dream that many people share is the dream of financial independence. This could mean different things to different people, but the idea is that they want to have enough money to live the life they want without worrying about finances. This dream motivates people to work hard, save money, and invest in their future.

Another example of a dream is the dream of starting a business. Many people have a passion for entrepreneurship and want to create something that has a positive impact on the world. This dream requires courage, hard work, and perseverance to turn it into a reality.

There are countless stories of individuals who achieved their dreams despite facing significant challenges and obstacles. For example, Oprah Winfrey, a media mogul, talk show host, and philanthropist, grew up in poverty and faced numerous setbacks throughout her life. However, her dream of becoming a media personality never wavered, and she persisted until she achieved her goals. Today, she is one of the most influential women in the world, and her success is a testament to the power of dreams.

Dreams are the starting point of all success in network marketing. Without dreams, there is no motivation to take action, no goals to work towards, and no vision for the future. Dreams are the fuel that drives us forward, and they are the foundation upon which all success is built.

The first step in building a successful network marketing business is to identify your dreams. What do you want to achieve? What is your ultimate goal? Do you want to achieve financial freedom, travel the world, or spend more time with your family? Whatever your dream may be, it is important to identify it and keep it at the forefront of your mind.

Once you have identified your dreams, the next step is to make a dream list. This is a list of all the things you want to achieve, experience, or acquire in your life. Your dream list can include anything from buying a new house or car, to traveling to a new country, to starting your own business. The key is to be specific and detailed about your dreams, and to write them down in a place where you can refer to them often.

Why is it important to make a dream list? Because your dreams serve as your compass, guiding you towards your ultimate goal. They give you a sense of purpose and direction, and provide you with the motivation and inspiration you need to take action and overcome obstacles.

One of the most inspiring stories of the power of dreams is that of J.K. Rowling, the author of the Harry Potter series. Before she became a bestselling author, Rowling was a struggling single mother living on welfare. However, she had a dream of becoming a writer, and she held onto that dream despite numerous rejections from publishers. Eventually, her persistence paid off, and she became one of the most successful authors of all time.

In network marketing, it is important to cultivate a mindset of abundance and possibility, and to believe that your dreams are achievable. Your dreams may seem daunting or even impossible at first, but with hard work, dedication, and a willingness to learn and grow, you can turn them into reality.

In conclusion, dreams are the foundation upon which all success is built in network marketing. By identifying your dreams and making a dream list, you can cultivate a mindset of abundance and possibility, and stay motivated and inspired as you work towards achieving your ultimate goal.

Here are some steps to make a dream list:

Set aside time: Find a quiet and comfortable place where you can focus on your thoughts without distractions. Dedicate at least an hour or two to this process.

Brainstorm: Start by brainstorming ideas for your dream list. Think about all the things you want to achieve in your life, both big and small. Don't worry about how achievable they are, just focus on your desires.

Write it down: Write down everything that comes to mind on a piece of paper or a digital document. Don't worry about organizing or prioritizing them yet.

Categorize: After you have brainstormed all of your ideas, start categorizing them. Group similar ideas together and create categories such as family, career, personal development, travel, financial, and more.

Prioritize: Once you have your dream list categorized, prioritize them based on what's most important to you. Ask yourself what dreams would have the most significant impact on your life and what you want to achieve first.

Revisit: Revisit your dream list frequently and update it as you achieve goals or as your desires change over time.

Take action: After creating your dream list, it's time to start taking action towards achieving them. Break down each dream into smaller achievable goals and take daily steps towards accomplishing them.

Remember that the dream list is a powerful tool to help you stay motivated and focused on your goals. It's essential to have a clear vision of what you want to achieve in life and business to succeed in network marketing.

CHAPTER 2

COMMITMENT

Commitment is one of the most essential building blocks of network marketing success. Without commitment, it is impossible to achieve your goals and dreams, and to build a thriving business. In this chapter, we will explore the importance of commitment in network marketing, and provide practical tips on how to cultivate a strong commitment to your business.

At its core, commitment is a decision to stick with something, even when it gets difficult or challenging. In network marketing, commitment means making a decision to build your business, and then taking consistent action towards that goal, day in and day out.

One of the key factors that separates successful network marketers from those who struggle is their level of commitment. Successful network marketers are committed to their business, and they do whatever it takes to achieve their goals. They are willing to put in the time and effort to learn and grow, to build relationships with their team and their customers, and to persevere through challenges and setbacks.

To cultivate a strong commitment to your network marketing

business, it is important to start by setting clear goals and defining your "why." Why are you building this business? What is your ultimate goal? What is driving you to take action and work towards success? By answering these questions and keeping your "why" at the forefront of your mind, you can stay motivated and inspired as you work towards your goals.

Another important aspect of commitment is accountability. It is important to have someone to hold you accountable for your actions and to keep you on track towards your goals. This can be a mentor, coach, or accountability partner who can provide guidance, support, and feedback as you work towards your goals.

Finally, it is important to celebrate your successes along the way, no matter how small they may be. Celebrating your successes can help you stay motivated and inspired, and can remind you of the progress you have made towards your goals.

In network marketing, commitment involves several aspects, including:

Time Commitment: Building a successful network marketing business takes time and effort. It requires consistent effort over an extended period. Being committed means dedicating enough time to the business, even if it means sacrificing other activities.

Financial Commitment: Network marketing may require a financial investment, such as buying products, attending events, or investing in training and personal development. A committed network marketer is willing to invest in their business and make financial sacrifices to achieve their goals.

Personal Development Commitment: Building a successful network marketing business requires developing skills such as communication, leadership, and sales. A committed network marketer is willing to learn, grow, and improve themselves continually.

Emotional Commitment: Network marketing can be challenging, and rejection can be discouraging. A committed network marketer has the mental fortitude to stay positive, resilient, and focused on their goals, despite the challenges they face.

In conclusion, commitment is an essential building block of network marketing success. By setting clear goals, defining your "why," staying accountable, and celebrating your successes, you can cultivate a strong commitment to your business, and achieve the success you desire.

CHAPTER 3

DR. IRFAN ASHRAF

NAME LIST

One of the first steps in building a successful network marketing business is to create a name list. Your name list is a list of people you know who may be interested in learning more about your business opportunity or products. In this chapter, we will explore why creating a name list is important, and provide tips on how to create a comprehensive and effective list.

Your name list is important because it is the foundation of your business. These are the people who will be your first customers, your first team members, and your first advocates. Without a strong name list, it will be difficult to get your business off the ground.

To create a comprehensive name list, start by brainstorming everyone you know, including family members, friends, coworkers, acquaintances, and people you have met through social or community groups. Don't leave anyone out, even if you don't think they would be interested in your business. You never know who might surprise you!

Once you have created your list, prioritize it by marking the people who you believe would be most interested in your business opportunity or products. These are the people you should focus on reaching out to first.

When reaching out to people on your name list, it is important to approach them in a non-salesy way. Instead of immediately pitching your business, start by building a relationship and getting to know them better. Ask questions about their interests and goals, and look for ways that your business can provide value to them.

Remember that building a successful network marketing business is all about building relationships and providing value to others. By creating a comprehensive name list and approaching people in a genuine and non-salesy way, you can build a strong foundation for your business and start building a successful team.

Here are some tips on creating a name list:

Start with People You Know: Begin by writing down the names of people you know, such as family members, friends, and acquaintances. These are people who are likely to know and trust you.

Think Outside Your Immediate Circle: Expand your list to include people you may not know well but who are within your social or professional networks, such as former classmates, co-workers', or neighbours.

Consider Referrals: Ask the people on your list if they know anyone who might be interested in your products or business opportunity. This can help you expand your network quickly.

Use Social Media: Use social media platforms such as Facebook and LinkedIn to identify potential prospects and add them to your list.

Keep Your List Organized: Use a spreadsheet or a notebook to keep your list organized and up to date. Include contact information, notes on the person's interests, and any other relevant information.

Creating a name list is crucial because it provides you with a starting point for building your network marketing business. Your list will be the foundation for your business, and the people on it will be the first ones you approach about your products or business opportunity. With a well-crafted name list and a commitment to taking consistent action, you can build a successful network marketing business.

CHAPTER 4

INVITATION AND THE ART OF PROSPECTING

Invitation and prospecting are two of the most important skills for success in network marketing. In this chapter, we will explore the art of prospecting, and provide tips on how to effectively invite people to learn more about your business opportunity.

Prospecting is the process of identifying and approaching people who may be interested in your business opportunity or products. To be successful at prospecting, it is important to approach people in a non-salesy way, and to focus on building relationships and providing value.

When approaching someone about your business opportunity, start by asking them questions about their goals and interests. This will help you to understand their needs and motivations, and to tailor your approach accordingly. Avoid using generic scripts or approaches, as these can come across as inauthentic and turn people off.

Once you have identified someone who may be interested in

your business opportunity, it is important to extend a genuine invitation to learn more. This could be an invitation to a meeting, a webinar, or a one-on-one conversation. Be clear about what you are inviting them to, and explain why you think it would be valuable for them to attend.

When extending an invitation, it is important to be respectful of people's time and boundaries. Don't be pushy or aggressive, and respect their decision if they decline your invitation. Remember that building a successful network marketing business is all about building relationships and providing value, not about pressuring people to join.

To be successful at prospecting, it is important to approach it as a long-term game. Don't expect to sign people up on the spot, and don't get discouraged if people say no. Instead, focus on building relationships and providing value, and trust that over time, people will become more interested in your business opportunity.

In conclusion, the art of prospecting is all about approaching people in a genuine and non-salesy way, and focusing on building relationships and providing value. By extending genuine invitations to learn more about your business opportunity, and approaching prospecting as a long-term game, you can build a successful network marketing business and help others achieve their goals.

Here are some tips on how to master the art of prospecting and inviting:

Start with Your Warm Market: Begin by reaching out to people you know, such as family members, friends, and acquaintances. These are people who are more likely to trust you and be receptive to your invitation.

Use a Script: Prepare a script or a set of talking points to guide your conversation when inviting someone. Your script should be simple, straightforward, and focused on the benefits of your products or business opportunity.

Be Genuine: Be sincere and authentic when reaching out to potential prospects. Show a genuine interest in them and their needs, and be willing to listen to their concerns.

Focus on the Benefits: Emphasize the benefits of your products or business opportunity and how they can help the prospect solve a problem or achieve a goal.

Use Multiple Channels: Use a variety of channels to reach out to potential prospects, such as phone calls, text messages, emails, social media, or in-person meetings.

Follow Up: Follow up with your prospects after your initial invitation. Follow-up shows that you care about their success and are committed to helping them achieve their goals.

Provide Value: Provide value to your prospects by sharing helpful information, tips, or resources related to your products or business opportunity. This can help you build trust and credibility with them.

By mastering the art of prospecting and inviting, you can build a robust network of customers and business partners, and grow your network marketing business. Remember, prospecting and inviting are skills that can be learned and developed with practice and persistence.

CHAPTER 5

PRESENTATION

Presentation is a critical component of network marketing, as it is the primary way to showcase your business opportunity and products to potential customers and team members. In this chapter, we will explore the key elements of a successful presentation, and provide tips on how to effectively communicate your message.

The first step in creating a successful presentation is to clearly define your message. What are the key benefits of your business opportunity and products? What makes them unique and valuable? These are the questions you need to answer in order to create a compelling and effective presentation.

Once you have defined your message, it is important to structure your presentation in a way that is easy to follow and understand. Start with an attention-grabbing introduction, and then move into the key benefits and features of your business opportunity and products. Be sure to provide specific examples and case studies to demonstrate the value of your offering.

In addition to the content of your presentation, it is also important to consider your delivery. Speak clearly and confidently, and use visual aids and other props to help illustrate your points. Be sure to engage your audience by asking questions and soliciting feedback, and be prepared to address any objections or concerns they may have.

Finally, it is important to personalize your presentation to the specific audience you are speaking to. Consider the goals and interests of your audience, and tailor your message accordingly. This will help to make your presentation more engaging and relevant to your audience, and increase the likelihood that they will be interested in learning more.

In conclusion, a successful presentation is all about clearly defining your message, structuring your presentation in an easy-to-follow way, delivering your message with confidence and engagement, and personalizing your message to your audience. By following these key principles, you can create a compelling and effective presentation that helps to build your business and attract potential customers and team members.

Here are some tips on how to create an effective presentation:

Keep it Simple: Keep your presentation simple and straightforward. Focus on the key benefits of your products or business opportunity, and avoid overwhelming your prospects with too much information.

Use Visual Aids: Use visual aids such as slides or videos to support your presentation. Visual aids can help you communicate your message more effectively and keep your prospects engaged.

Tell a Story: Use storytelling to make your presentation more compelling and memorable. Share stories of how your products or business opportunity have helped others achieve success or overcome challenges.

Address Objections: Address common objections that your prospects may have, such as price or time commitment, and provide solutions to these objections.

Include a Call to Action: Include a clear call to action at the end of your presentation. This can be a request for a follow-up meeting, a request for a purchase, or an invitation to join your business opportunity.

Practice, Practice, Practice: Practice your presentation until you feel comfortable and confident delivering it. Rehearse in front of a mirror or with a friend or family member.

Customize Your Presentation: Customize your presentation for each prospect, taking into account their specific needs and interests.

Remember, an effective presentation is a key element of building a successful network marketing business. With practice and persistence, you can create a compelling presentation that inspires your prospects to take action.

CHAPTER 6

FOLLOW THROUGH

Follow through is a critical element in the success of any network marketing business. It involves maintaining contact with your prospects and team members, and following up on any promises or commitments you have made. In this chapter, we will explore the key elements of effective follow through, and provide tips on how to keep your business moving forward.

The first step in effective follow through is to establish clear goals and timelines. Define what you want to achieve, and set specific deadlines for achieving these goals. This will help to keep you focused and motivated, and ensure that you are taking consistent action to build your business.

Once you have established your goals and timelines, it is important to stay organized and track your progress. Use a planner or calendar to schedule follow up calls and meetings with your prospects and team members, and keep detailed notes on your conversations and interactions. This will help to ensure that you are staying on track, and that you are not forgetting any important details or commitments.

In addition to staying organized, it is also important to be persistent and consistent in your follow through. Don't give up after the first rejection or obstacle, and don't let a lack of response from your prospects or team members discourage you. Keep reaching out and following up, and stay committed to building your business over the long term.

Finally, it is important to be responsive and attentive to the needs of your prospects and team members. Listen carefully to their concerns and questions, and provide timely and helpful responses. This will help to build trust and credibility, and increase the likelihood that they will be interested in working with you over the long term.

In conclusion, effective follow through is all about establishing clear goals and timelines, staying organized and tracking your progress, being persistent and consistent, and being responsive and attentive to the needs of your prospects and team members. By following these key principles, you can build a strong and successful network marketing business that helps you achieve your goals and dreams.

Here are some tips on how to master follow-through:

Set Expectations: Set clear expectations with your customers and business partners, and ensure that you deliver on your promises. This can help you build trust and credibility with them.

Stay in Touch: Maintain regular communication with your customers and business partners, even if it's just a quick check-in. This can help you stay top of mind and keep them engaged.

Provide Support: Provide ongoing support to your customers and business partners. Offer guidance, resources, and training to help them achieve their goals and overcome challenges.

Be Responsive: Be responsive to your customers and business partners' needs and concerns. Respond promptly to their inquiries and address their questions and issues in a timely and professional manner.

Celebrate Success: Celebrate your customers and business partners' success and achievements. Recognize their efforts and accomplishments, and show them that you appreciate their hard work.

Keep Learning: Continuously learn and improve your skills and knowledge in network marketing. Stay up-to-date with industry trends and best practices, and seek out opportunities for professional development.

By mastering follow-through, you can build strong, long-lasting relationships with your customers and business partners and grow your network marketing business. Remember, success in network marketing requires consistent effort, dedication, and a commitment to providing value to your customers and business partners.

CHAPTER 7

COUNSEL WITH YOUR UPLINE

One of the key benefits of network marketing is the support and guidance provided by your upline, or the individuals who have sponsored you into the business. In this chapter, we will explore the importance of seeking counsel from your upline, and how to effectively communicate with them to build a successful business.

First and foremost, it is important to establish a strong relationship with your upline. This means regularly communicating with them, attending meetings and events, and being open to feedback and guidance. Your upline has likely been through many of the same challenges and obstacles that you will face, and can provide valuable insights and advice on how to overcome them.

When seeking counsel from your upline, it is important to be clear about your goals and challenges. Explain what you are trying to achieve, and what specific challenges or obstacles you are facing. This will help your upline provide targeted advice and guidance that is tailored to your unique situation.

In addition to seeking advice and guidance, it is also important to learn from your upline's experience and expertise. Attend training sessions and webinars, read books and articles they recommend, and ask for recommendations on resources that can help you build your skills and knowledge.

Finally, it is important to be open to feedback and willing to make changes to your approach based on your upline's guidance. This may involve adjusting your goals or strategies, or making changes to your mindset or approach. Remember, your upline's advice and guidance is based on years of experience and success in the industry, and can help you achieve your own success as well.

In conclusion, seeking counsel from your upline is an essential element of building a successful network marketing business. By establishing a strong relationship, being clear about your goals and challenges, learning from their experience and expertise, and being open to feedback and making changes, you can build a strong and successful business that helps you achieve your goals and dreams.

Here are some tips on how to effectively counsel with your upline:

Schedule Regular Check-Ins: Schedule regular check-ins with your upline, whether it's weekly, bi-weekly, or monthly. This can help you stay on track and receive guidance and support as you navigate your business.

Be Open and Honest: Be open and honest with your upline about your goals, challenges, and concerns. This can help them provide you with relevant and personalized advice.

Seek Feedback: Ask your upline for feedback on your progress and performance. This can help you identify areas for improvement and take corrective action.

Attend Training and Events: Attend training sessions, webinars, and events hosted by your upline. This can help you learn new skills, connect with other network marketers, and gain fresh perspectives on your business.

Embrace Constructive Criticism: Be open to constructive criticism from your upline. Use their feedback as an opportunity to learn and grow in your business.

Remember, your upline can be a valuable resource in your network marketing journey. By counseling with them regularly, you can gain valuable insights and guidance that can help you achieve success in your business.

CHAPTER 8

DUPLICATION

One of the most important aspects of network marketing is duplication. Duplication is the process of teaching and training others to do what you do, so that they can build their own successful businesses. In this chapter, we will explore the importance of duplication and how to effectively duplicate your success with others.

Duplication is essential for the growth and success of your network marketing business. Without duplication, you will be limited by your own time and efforts, and your income potential will be capped. By teaching and training others to do what you do, you can leverage the efforts of many people and exponentially grow your business.

To effectively duplicate your success, it is important to have a clear and duplicable system in place. This system should include a step-by-step process for building the business, training materials and resources, and support from your upline and other leaders in the organization. By having a clear and duplicable system, you can ensure that everyone in your organization is working towards the same goals and using the same strategies for success.

In addition to having a clear system, it is important to lead by example and set a positive and enthusiastic tone for your team. By consistently demonstrating your own success and sharing your enthusiasm and passion for the business, you can inspire and motivate others to achieve their own success.

Finally, it is important to consistently communicate with and support your team members. This includes providing ongoing training and education, offering encouragement and feedback, and recognizing and celebrating their successes. By providing consistent support and guidance, you can help your team members stay motivated and committed to their goals.

In conclusion, duplication is essential for building a successful network marketing business. By having a clear and duplicable system in place, leading by example, and consistently communicating with and supporting your team members, you can effectively duplicate your success and help others achieve their goals and dreams.

Here are some tips on how to effectively duplicate your success:

Create a Simple System: Create a simple, step-by-step system that can be easily replicated by others. This can help you attract and retain more people in your network marketing organization.

Lead by Example: Lead by example and model the behaviours and actions that you want others to follow. This can help you establish credibility and inspire others to take action.

Provide Training and Support: Provide training and support to your team members to help them succeed. This can include one-on-one coaching, group training sessions, and access to resources and tools.

Encourage Action: Encourage your team members to take action and implement the strategies and tactics that you teach them. This can help them gain confidence and achieve success.

Recognize and Reward: Recognize and reward your team members for their achievements and successes. This can help motivate them and create a positive, supportive team culture.

Remember, duplication is essential for building a successful network marketing business. By creating a simple, replicable system and providing training and support to your team members, you can help them achieve their goals and create a thriving organization.

DR. IRFAN ASHRAF

CONCLUSION

I n conclusion, network marketing and direct selling offer a unique and rewarding opportunity to build a successful business and achieve your dreams. By focusing on the eight basic building blocks of network marketing - dreams, commitment, name list, invitation and the art of prospecting, presentation, follow through, counsel with your upline, and duplication - you can build a strong and sustainable business that can provide financial and personal fulfilment.

Remember to keep your dreams at the forefront of your mind and use them as motivation to keep pushing forward. Be committed to your business and invest the time and effort needed to make it successful. Use your name list and effective prospecting techniques to build a strong network of contacts and potential customers. Master the art of presentation and follow through with your prospects to convert them into customers or business partners.

Additionally, always seek guidance and support from your upline and other leaders in your organization. They can provide valuable insights, training, and support to help you achieve your goals.

Finally, focus on duplication to expand your network and leverage the efforts of others. By teaching and training others to do what you do, you can exponentially grow your business and help others achieve their dreams as well.

With these building blocks in place, you can create a successful and fulfilling network marketing business that allows you to live the life of your dreams.

Here are some key points to remember from the e-book on the eight basic building blocks of network marketing:

Dreams: Your dreams are the foundation of your motivation and should guide your actions and decisions in your network marketing business.

Commitment: Network marketing requires commitment and effort to be successful, and you should be prepared to invest time and energy in your business.

Name List: Your name list is a crucial starting point for building your network and should include everyone you know or have interacted with.

Invitation and the Art of Prospecting: Inviting and prospecting are essential skills for growing your network and should be done with sincerity and authenticity.

Presentation: A strong and effective presentation can be the difference between converting a prospect into a customer or business partner or losing them altogether.

Follow Through: Following up with your prospects is essential for building relationships and converting them into customers

or business partners.

Counsel with Your Upline: Seeking guidance and support from your upline and other leaders can provide valuable insights and training to help you achieve your goals.

Duplication: Duplication is the process of teaching and training others to do what you do, and is essential for leveraging the efforts of others and building a sustainable business.

By focusing on these key points and consistently implementing them in your network marketing business, you can build a strong and successful business that can provide financial and personal fulfilment.